The Entrepreneur's Guide to Cannabis:

Concentrated Advice From 25 Industry Leaders

D1360308

Michael Zaytsev

ISBN: 1535285958
ISBN-13: 978-1535285957

Thank you to all my family, friends, mentors, coaches and to the High NY community. Thank you for your support along this beautiful journey. You inspire me to be the highest possible version of myself.

This book is dedicated to the Cannabis prisoners, the medical patients, the casualties of the War on Drugs, and any of their loved ones who have been hurt by Prohibition.

Enough is enough. Free the herb.

CONTENTS

Introduction   8

1   Business as Usual   15

2   Unlike Anything Ever Before   24

3   Activism Mandatory   30

4   Ancillary or Nah?   38

5   Long Term Focus   41

6   What's Your One Thing?   43

7   Expect Change   46

8   Embrace Failure   47

9   There's Enough Green for Everyone   50

10 Most Importantly: People & Results   53

    The Future of the Cannabis Industry   62

    Appendix: Meet the Leaders   70

    About the Author   84

INTRODUCTION

The legalization of the Cannabis industry is the biggest opportunity for entrepreneurship since the birth of the Internet— *If not bigger!* I am grateful to be able to participate and am excited that you're considering doing the same.

As the founder of High NY, the largest community of Cannabis activists and entrepreneurs in New York, I've created educational events and content that have sparked thousands of conversations about Cannabis. High NY has incubated businesses, advocated for patients, and has empowered local leaders to succeed in their startups. Our members have been featured in *TechCrunch*, *Fortune*, and the *New York Times*. Along with High NY, I have been featured in *The Guardian, The New York Post, Complex, Village Voice, Mic, Inc., Vice, Timeout New York, Crain's, Mashable, Merry Jane* and more for my work in the Cannabis community.

If you're thinking about starting a cannabis business I want to help you succeed. Why? Partially, because I love the plant. Partially, because I believe entrepreneurship is one of the best vehicles for positive social impact. And, largely, it is because this industry is in need of talented, passionate people who are willing to fight for justice. For those reasons, I've devoted the last 2 years of my life to serving the Cannabis community. This book, however, is not about me. It's all about you. And the plant, the industry, and the future we all share together.

When I entered the Cannabis industry— organizing education and networking events in New York City— I used the sales skills I learned working at Google to connect with industry leaders and interview them on advice for succeeding as a Cannabis entrepreneur. Over the last 2 years, I've been fortunate enough to learn from and partner with some world-class leaders. Among these are people who will no doubt get lots of ink in the history books as Cannabis champions: Steve DeAngelo, Ethan Nadelmann, Dana Beal, Betty Aldworth, Jason Pinsky, Robert Calkin, Jack Cole, Dr. Sue Sisley, some OG's that won't be named and many more.

These are business people, activists, medical professionals and above all, people who have been dedicated to creating a world free from Cannabis prohibition and the many dangers associated with it. I am grateful for their work. I truly am standing on the shoulders of giants. Without them, this book would not exist.

About This Book

This book is intended to do to one thing: **create more successful Cannabis leaders and entrepreneurs.** It is meant to be a resource for any entrepreneur looking to enter legal Cannabis. Mostly, it is aimed at those who are beginner entrepreneurs but experienced with Cannabis, or those who are experienced entrepreneurs but are beginners when it comes to Cannabis. **My goal is to give you 1,000% ROI (return on investment) with this book**. So if it takes an hour to read and brainstorm all the questions and challenges I present, I want this book to create enough value to save you 10 hours of frustration —or worse, inaction— with your Cannabis business.

When I entered the industry, a book like this simply did not exist. In fact, until I wrote this book, a book like this did not exist. I have interviewed some of the movement's top leaders and asked for their best advice for entrepreneurs who want to be in Cannabis. **This book is the result of 2 years of full immersion and hard work.** And because I did it, you don't have to.

There's No Better Time Than Now To Enter The Cannabis Industry.

Well, except yesterday. Or last year. You get the point. The sooner you start, the sooner you can reach your goals. Plus, the greater your chance of having a first mover advantage. I am often asked whether or not it is too late to enter the industry. The answer is a resounding **FUCK NO!** Is it too late to open a restaurant? Or start a clothing brand? No. Cannabis has been around forever and will be around forever. There will always be demand for it. Thus, it will never be too late.

As a thank you for picking up this book and investing in your skills and by extension the Cannabis industry, I'm going to share with you some of my favorite resources for any entrepreneur thinking about starting a company.

****ATTENTION****

Special Offer

BEFORE YOU CONTINUE:

Go to Entrepreneur420.com/BONUS to get a bunch of free additional resources including examples of successful ancillary businesses, videos of the expert interviews, recommended reading lists, and more. You can also download the audiobook for free @
www.ENTREPRENEUR420.com/BONUS

In the spirit of transparency, I must share my other motivations for writing this book.

Paying it Forward

Each of the people whom I interviewed is a busy, "important" person (every person is an important person, but I won't get stoner philosophical on you). They've got things to do and places to be. Yet they all took the time to speak with me, educate me and share their wisdom. Now that I'm in a position where I can help facilitate the growth of other leaders and entrepreneurs, I feel an obligation to do so. This book allows me to do that at scale.

It's Good Business

I am confident that after you read it you will get more than your money's worth. This book will allow me to provide value for all the folks I interviewed, because I'm creating another channel through which their work is showcased www.Entrepreneur420.com/Leaders. Win-win-win. Yes! Also, there is no book like this for the aspiring Cannabis entrepreneur. As an entrepreneur myself, the opportunity to address a gap in the marketplace is simply too good to pass up.

We Share Success

As I discuss in Chapter 9, this industry is big enough for everyone. Even a small business in a $50 Billion dollar industry can become a multi-million dollar enterprise. There's plenty of room for competition in this industry. In fact, it's the sign of a healthy industry! As the industry expands, the Cannabis lifestyle becomes more socially accepted, patients get access to quality medicine, and our broken criminal justice system gets reformed. That's the impact I want to drive.

THE GROWTH OF THE INDUSTRY IS ACCELERATING: THE CANNABIS INDUSTRY WILL NEVER AGAIN BE AS SMALL AS IT IS TODAY!

Just 18 months ago, I didn't know ANYTHING about Cannabis other than how to consume it. Today, I lead High NY, one of the world's largest Cannabis Meetup groups, and I have built a network of really terrific, inspiring and talented industry leaders. *If I can do it, you can too.* The only tools I used to create all this were a laptop, cell phone, time, effort, and Cannabis.

I want to do my best to help you and if you have any specific questions or think I may be able to assist you, or if I've made a mistake somewhere please email me **Mike@Entrepreneur420.com**.

After reading this book you will have a more complete understanding of what it takes to build a successful Cannabis business. I hope the book will inspire you towards bold, courageous action. **If the Cannabis plant is important to you and you're inspired to give back to the plant and the community, then know this: not only is there room for you in this industry, but also this industry needs your talent!**

"Have fun and enjoy it."
Scott Reach

1.
Business as Usual

"My advice to Cannabis entrepreneurs, or to any entrepreneurs, is to follow your passion. Creating a new business is an incredibly challenging and difficult thing: it will demand all of your time and attention, there will be a lot of heartache along the way, and you will have to endure through many difficult moments. If you don't have a real passion to do what it is that you're doing, it's going to be very difficult to persevere. Follow your passion, develop a good plan and a good team —the money and success will follow." **-Steve DeAngelo**

"Have a unique vision, a differentiated strategy, and make sure you're approaching the problem you're intending to solve, not only with conviction, but also with data."
-Evan Eneman

It doesn't matter if you're talking about Cannabis, cotton candy, construction, or corn flakes, capitalism follows certain rules. Supply and demand, competition, free cash flow, intellectual property, customer service. These aren't just concepts, these are realities that every entrepreneur must continuously be aware of. What is an entrepreneur? There are plenty of definitions I can offer, but none can capture the dynamic nature of the role. One thing I can tell you with absolute certainty is this: **Entrepreneurship is fucking difficult!**

Being your own boss and creating a sustainable, profitable business are difficult undertakings. Cannabis is becoming more competitive and complex by the second. If you believe in history and statistics, then it might upset you to learn that the expected outcome of starting a business is failure. More than half of all new businesses are out-of-business within 5 years. Imagine busting your ass for 5 years only to shut down shop. Approaching challenges like that on daily basis with a level of "FUCK YES!" enthusiasm is the bare minimum grit required to be a successful entrepreneur.

So why do it? Maybe you sense that this industry is the greatest opportunity for entrepreneurship (and profit) in your lifetime. Or perhaps the chance to participate in shaping a major global market excites you. Or maybe you know that the old model is completely broken, outdated and you're ready to give up your 9-5 indentured servitude. Maybe you just love Cannabis and want to build a career around it. Whatever the case may be, I commend you for investing in your education and skills by picking up this book.

Entrepreneur is a *mindset* made up of *powerful habits* expressed through *energetic execution* all built on a *foundation of values, integrity and determination*. It's important and rewarding work. **But at the end of the day, business is business**. It's dollars and cents. Does your business make sense? Does it make dollars?

Below are 5 fundamentals that any professional investor will evaluate before investing in a company:

1) Team

○ Who is on your team?

○ Are they trustworthy, coachable and experienced?

2) Value Proposition

○ What problem does your product or service solve?

○ What value does your product or service create?

○ Can you prove it?

3) Business Model

○ How does it scale?

○ How can you build a system to consistently monetize the product or service?

○ Are your valuations grounded in reality?

○ Have you detailed the risks inherent to your model?

4) The Entrepreneur's Understanding of Market Dynamics

○ Do you know the industry players?

○ How is the industry evolving?

○ What direction are we heading in?

○ How will your company adapt and deal with uncertainty?

○ What systematic or industry risk are you vulnerable to?

○ What do you know that nobody else knows?

5) Exit / ROI

○ What is the exit opportunity?

○ How will the investor make his or her money back?

○ How long will it take?

○ What size return can they expect?

Next are some questions for you to seriously consider before starting your venture.

- Who is your customer and what value are you providing them?

- Does your product or service exist already?

Why or why not?

- What problem does it solve? How valuable is solving that problem?

- How much will it cost to create your product or service?

- How can you test that people will pay for your goods or service?

- How will you sell and market it?

- How does it scale?

Or asked bluntly, how does your business make money? If these questions sound like no brainers for you, great, take action to test the answers you've come up with. If these questions aren't ones you've considered, then perhaps you may want to invest some time to educate yourself about entrepreneurship.

For my list of top resources for entrepreneurship education visit ***Entrepreneur420.com/bonus***

"If you don't have a background in entrepreneurship, start there. If you've already got the business basics down —how your accounting works, how your business plan works— then dive deeply into the Cannabis industry. Talk to everybody. This is an industry that was underground for

years and years. The information isn't all available online. Talk to people on the ground to understand where this industry is going." **-Jazmin Hupp**

Entrepreneurship is a dance: there are rules, routines and rhythms. The art and science of business goes back many generations. Reading is one of my daily success habits; it gives me access to some of the greatest business minds of all time.

Reading and learning are great, but **entrepreneurship is about action.** The #1 factor of your success, which is within your control, is execution. Even when you're pursuing a purpose with passion and powerful motivation, effort still takes effort. Just do it! Imperfect action is often more productive than analyzing and strategizing to find the "optimal solution." Let the market validate your business. Get feedback from your clients. Constantly improve your offering.

Success is the result of strong daily habits — both physical and psychological. Why? Because great habits create great behaviors which create great outcomes. And great outcomes compound. Habit #2 of Stephen Covey's *7 Habits of Highly Successful People* is to "begin with the end in mind." Be aware of your goals and make sure the actions you are taking bring you closer to achieving those goals.

Applied more broadly, **what do you want to accomplish by starting a business?** What's the exit? Are you looking to get acquired? Are you building an empire? Is passive income the goal? Or a lifestyle business that allows you lots of free time to enjoy leisure and hobbies? This clarity of purpose will help you motivate yourself to fight through the tough challenges that you will undoubtedly encounter on your entrepreneur's journey.

Cannabis Education

How much do you know about Cannabis? Have you grown the plant? Do you know why it became illegal? How much do you know about the power of Cannabis medicine? Or safe consumption? There are several resources you can take advantage of to increase your Cannabis IQ: here are some of my favorite reference materials in no particular order.

- *The Cannabis Manifesto* by Steve DeAngelo
- *Marijuana Grower's Handbook* and *Beyond Buds* by Ed Rosenthal
- *Hemp Bound* by Doug Fine
- *The Emperor Wears No Clothes* by Jack Herer
- The Weed Blog
- ProjectCBD

- Leafly
- Oaksterdam University, The Cannabis Career Institute, Cloverleaf University all offer classes
- Green Flower Media and the Holistic Cannabis Network host virtual education conferences and provide great free content
- Drug Policy Alliance
- Marijuana Policy Project
- Students for Sensible Drug Policy
- Americans for Safe Access
- NORML
- Freedom Leaf
- Law Enforcement Against Prohibition
- Search for academic journal articles on Google Scholar

I began my work in Cannabis because I loved the plant and was absolutely appalled when I learned the ugly truth about its prohibition; the fact that so many people were being robbed of health benefits and healing because of bad policy; that so many people had their freedom stolen and lives ruined because of possession arrests (and skin tone); and the fact that this plant has been used by people for thousands of years, and has become illegal even though it is a gift from Mother Earth. Those things pissed me off so much that I knew if I dedicated my life to improving the status quo, it would be a life worth living.

One Piece of Advice

Enjoy. The hard work, challenges, and growth you're about to experience are huge wins. Entrepreneurship, when done correctly, is the highest paying job humanly possible. Your earnings potential is limited only by your imagination and ability to manifest it. Learning is constant. And in Cannabis, you'll meet colorful, inspired, fascinating people. Enjoy. Celebrate the small (and big) wins along the way and the opportunity to try. It takes a lot of courage to start a business. Be proud of your bravery.

Build. Test. Prove. Improve. Scale. Repeat. But before you begin, know this: the Cannabis industry is unlike anything ever seen before.

2.

Unlike Anything Ever Before

"You don't know what you're getting into. You need to have the Love for what you're doing to succeed. I wouldn't recommend someone who's not into Cannabis to get into the Cannabis industry." **-Rhory Gould**

"There is no cannabis industry or market — there are 25 separated markets and each one must be treated differently."
-Alain Bankier

This is a unique, unprecedented opportunity for entrepreneurs to take advantage of. It's the biggest thing since the birth of dot com. This industry represents more than $50 Billion dollars *annually*. But the truth is, nobody knows what's going to happen.

This isn't like alcohol prohibition ending. Alcohol was legal just a few years prior to the failed prohibition experiment. Cannabis is different. It hasn't been legal in almost a century. Besides, alcohol is truly a vice product. Cannabis is significantly more versatile. In fact, I believe that Cannabis medicine, Cannabis for personal use, and non psychoactive Hemp represent entirely different industries, and must be regulated separately.

Cannabis is unique:

1) A commodity with multi-billion dollar demand is considered federally illegal, yet is legal in half of the United States. Each state's legal market has completely different regulations and rules. As of the writing of this book, there are 25 U.S. states in which Cannabis is legal. Each one has unique regulatory environments, market dynamics, and players.

2) There is direct competition with the black market.

3) Consumers are vastly under-informed, overly forgiving and used to purchasing goods illegally.

4) Decades of anti-Cannabis propaganda must be undone. There is a very real stigma against Cannabis. Imagine if you grew up being told the internet or smart phones were evil or dangerous. Or that coffee would ruin your life and you shouldn't drink it.

5) Business owners and investors are not able to access banking resources. Millions of dollars in transactions —paying taxes, salaries, business expenses— happen in cash.

6) The majority of people who run this industry are "stoners." While this is mostly fun, as several business meetings include, or rather necessitate, consumption, it also presents certain challenges. But mostly, it's just fun.

7) B2B Technology and infrastructure that other industries have enjoyed over the past few decades are just now being developed and made available in Cannabis.

8) It is illegal and very difficult to advertise the product around which the industry revolves. Facebook, Google, TV, and most other mainstream marketing channels do not allow the advertisement of a federally illegal narcotic.

9) Industrial Hemp: with over 20,000 documented uses, the non psychoactive variety of Cannabis has the potential to significantly disrupt the food, energy, materials, and clothing industries.

10) Section 280E of the federal tax code severely limits the expenses businesses that produce, process, or sell Cannabis are able to write off. This creates an environment in which businesses pay an effective tax rate of 70% or higher. That rate is absolutely unheard of in other industries.

"No deduction or credit shall be allowed for any amount paid or incurred during the taxable year in carrying on any trade or business if such trade or business (or the activities which comprise such trade or business) consists of trafficking in controlled substances (within the meaning of schedule I and II of the Controlled Substances Act) which is prohibited by Federal law or the law of any State in which such trade or business is conducted."

11) Speaking of laws, **the laws and regulations are unpredictable and ever changing.** Uncertainty is constant.

Anyone who says they have a lens into the future is more likely than not to be wrong. We're still in the very early stages of a multi-billion dollar global industry being set up. *This industry does not even have access to banking yet*! Producers and processors in Colorado, Washington, Oregon, etc. are paying their taxes in straight cash, homie.

"This is a new market emerging from the black market, there's nothing like it. Make sure you're dealing with people who are genuine and experienced. Find out where your investors' money is coming from."
-Larisa Bolivar

Let's be clear, **Cannabis is not a new industry, but *legal* Cannabis is in its infancy.** The black market for Cannabis is a multi billion dollar global industry. There are established players, values, "corporate" culture, relationship dynamics, history and more. There are people who have been risking their freedom for decades in Cannabis business. State by state there are transitions from black to gray to regulated legal markets. Brand new actors are entering this space every day.

Given these circumstances, it's especially important in Cannabis to **know who you're dealing with** (the puns are *always* intended). The reality of any rapidly growing industry is that it will attract opportunistic people who are interested in making money. You will encounter people who are willing to lie, cheat, and steal (or worse) their way to wealth. Be extra careful about who you work with and make sure you have an experienced lawyer whom you trust.

When has a product ever come to market after nearly a century of misinformation?

Cannabis is consumed daily by millions of people. Yet the vast majority of them are grossly under informed about the plant, how it affects them, and what they're putting into their bodies. Since the 1930's, infamous prohibitionists like Henry Anslinger, Richard Nixon, Ronald Reagan, and their cronies have done a terribly effective job of brainwashing people into thinking Cannabis is really, really dangerous. Today, many people still believe that the plant is a gateway drug. Most American adults grew up being told that this is a dangerous drug that will fry your brain, get you hooked, and ruin your life.

Thanks to the internet and activism, more and more people know that the propaganda is bullshit. However, it still creates a unique business dynamic. Banks do not work with Cannabis companies because the plant is a federally illegal narcotic. Some people will consider you a drug dealer or drug user for being in the Cannabis industry. **The stoner stigma is real, but it is shifting**.

Public perception is hugely important in affecting policy changes. Today, more than 60% of Americans support Cannabis legalization; however, this does not change the fact that most are severely undereducated about the realities of the plant. Many of them have heard the propaganda countless times and have never questioned it. So if you're looking to enter this industry, you must be prepared to educate yourself and then educate others who are not familiar with the history and reality of the plant. Ignorance is bad for business.

3.
Activism Mandatory

"The War on Drugs is a self perpetuating, constantly expanding policy disaster. Every year it's worse than the year before. We've been making it worse now for the last 45 years. We've spent more than $1.5 trillion on this war. All we've got to show for that is this —we've made 50 million arrests for nonviolent drug offenses. Think about that, some countries don't have 50 million people. And we've done everything we can possibly do to destroy the lives of the people we arrest." **-Jack Cole**

"If you are looking to benefit from this industry, acknowledge the fact that Cannabis prohibition has been destroying lives for nearly a century now. Remember where this is coming from. Communities of color and low income communities have suffered from prohibition disproportionately more than any other [group]."
-Betty Aldworth

"Don't assume it's in the bag. Cannabis isn't going to legalize itself. It's not

inevitable. We're in a very real, very tough political battle and it is far from over."
-Ethan Nadelmann

What values do you want to bring to this industry? Robert Raich, who took two landmark Cannabis cases to the Supreme Court, compares this industry to a rocket ship lifting off. Just a few millimeters off target right now can launch us into the wrong universe 15 or 50 years from now. Why? Because if we don't correct the social injustices of prohibition with sensible and fair laws —or worse— if we allow bad policy to prevail, we can end up in another disastrous situation.

Millions of lives have been unjustly ruined by Cannabis prohibition. A disproportionately large segment of those have been young men of color who are victims of a system created to serve racist, evil agendas. Who will advocate on behalf of the people with criminal records and limited options to make an honest living? Or those still in jail? Who will lobby on behalf of those disadvantaged people? How will those people who have lost their liberties be made whole?

What about all the sick people who are prevented from access to safe, natural medicine? How come the government makes it so difficult to research this plant's medical properties? How can we take advantage of this plant to make advances in public health? When you consider chronic pain, cancer, Alzheimer's, epilepsy, ADHD, HIV and PTSD, there are millions of people around the world who can benefit from whole-plant Cannabis medicine. Who is going to advocate and lobby on behalf of these sick people? How much would society benefit from a more healthy population? Seriously, why are there so many barriers to research? Guess who owns one of the only patents on Cannabinoid medicine? I'll give you a hint, it's the U.S.A's Federal Government.

What gives the government the right to control what we do with our bodies? Isn't it every human's natural born right to alter his consciousness? After all, Cannabis is just a plant. It comes from the Earth. And let's not even get into hemp and its 20,000+ potential uses. Superfood, biofuel, clothing, and building material to name a few. What would happen to our dependence on fossil fuels and industrial meat farming if we embraced hemp?

How do laws get changed in your state?

By ballot initiative or referendum? What legislation has been proposed in your state? Have you voiced your opinions to your elected officials? Is there a local organization educating politicians about Cannabis? Who is helping patients in your community? What are the attitudes of local health care providers?

Change comes from the bottom up. Community boards, city councils, state legislatures, congress members, union leaders and, of course, donors. These are just some of the characters that play a role in political reform. Being a productive Cannabis citizen requires being a productive citizen. **For laws to change AND BE WRITTEN IN A WAY THAT PROTECT CANNABIS VALUES, passionate, educated people MUST engage in the political process.** Organizations like Marijuana Policy Project, Students for Sensible Drug Policy, Americans for Safe Access, and Drug Policy Alliance are leading the charge on a national level. Get familiar with the work they're doing and how you can contribute. And, of course, vote!

Who is paying the lobbyists and greasing the wheels of democracy so that laws are written a certain way? The failed legalization attempt in Ohio demonstrates that the people who really care about the plant will defend it from greedy corporate interests who simply seek new revenue streams. However, it also demonstrated that if left unchecked, profiteers will exploit the system to create legal monopolies or oligopolies. In fact, the argument can easily be made that one reason Cannabis became illegal in the first place was to protect the corporate interests of people who knew that hemp would challenge their empires.

Without the work of activists and advocates who have driven the grassroots fight for Cannabis freedom, *there would not be a legal Cannabis industry today.* Pay your respects, but also step up and do your part.

If you have not contributed to the activism required to free the plant, then you don't deserve to profit from the boom. That's just my opinion. But I'm willing to bet a lot of OG's and industry leaders who have risked their freedom and well being for decades would agree with me.

The legal Cannabis industry is a gateway revolution.

It will create subsequent revolutions. It will transform medicine, agriculture, government, business and much more. This is what makes the industry so incredibly exciting. $50 Billion dollars, a change of federal law, the transition from black to legal market, a renewed interest in plants, a new type of industry where diversity and gender equality are established up front. We do not know how these paradigm shifts will play out years from now, but there is no doubt that they will set off many other reactions that nobody can fully anticipate.

"Most of the successful people in the industry right now are interested in this thing beyond money, they're really down for the cause and are activists." -**Ben Polarra**

If you're not ready to commit to Cannabis activism, you should seriously consider whether or not Cannabis entrepreneurship is right for you. A commitment to activism demonstrates a commitment to Cannabis culture and an interest in the industry that extends beyond financial gain. To be clear, there's nothing wrong with seeking financial gain. However, if you really want to achieve a high level of success in Cannabis, consider this: most of the top people are not primarily motivated by money.

Understanding 'The Cause'

"Stay focused on what you're fighting for. It's not an easy fight. Stay focused on the core values that drive us all. It's not about you. It's about the greater good. It doesn't matter who gets the credit, it's about people getting life saving medicine, and people not losing their freedoms and futures to the War on Drugs." -**Charlo Greene**

Now this is speculation, but my gut tells me that the people who have been running this industry for the past few decades care a lot about personal freedom. Specifically, a human being's right to enhance his own consciousness or to grow a plant of her choosing. Money likely is not the #1 thing that drives them to do the work they do. If you want relationships with the power players in this industry, the best of the best, you better have proof that you're down for the cause.

Cannabis is a plant. It offers numerous benefits. Humans should be free to grow a plant. Furthermore, a lot of the OG's have friends who won't get to prosper in legal Cannabis. Why? Because they were prospering during the times of illegal Cannabis. Some of these people have done time because of their involvement in the industry. This is something that should be treated with respect and discretion. Honor people's pasts without passing judgment. *But use your judgment about their character!*

Due to the illicit history of this industry, you will encounter criminals who are only driven by personal financial gain. You will also encounter people with criminal records, yet who are some of the kindest, most honest people you can possibly do business with. And of course, you'll encounter everyone in between.

There is still a big disconnect between how

Cannabis is perceived by the average person and the realities of the plant. Often, people who are unfamiliar with it are critical even though they have very little actual knowledge. Although there's no stigma against being an entrepreneur, there are still many people who are uncomfortable with entrepreneurship as they know little about this sometimes seemingly mystical profession.

If your path is anything like mine — transitioning from employee in corporate America to entrepreneur in Cannabis— people are going to look at you sideways. Not only will you be criticized for being unconventional and taking control of your life, but you will also be condescended for choosing to work in Cannabis. Be prepared to hear stupid jokes about being a Cannabis entrepreneur. This comes with the territory. Just view it as another opportunity to exercise your grit and mental toughness muscles.

On the flip side, there will be people who find your work fascinating, exciting and will want to know all about your Cannabis career. That's great, enjoy those moments, and make sure you take the opportunity to educate people about the plant and the impact it has. **You have an obligation to be a productive Cannabis citizen.**

4.
Ancillary or Nah?

Different types of Cannabis businesses

"Think outside the box. We're building a new industry from scratch. We have the chance to create a new type of industry, not just follow the old models. -**Rachelle Yeung**

The answer to this question should be automatic. This is something you've got to be trichome crystal clear on. Ask potential investors, employees, and partners this question. It's either one or the other. Do you want to be on the product side of this industry —growing, extracting, cooking, distributing— or not?

People excited by the Cannabis industry commonly ask, "how do I open a dispensary?" Depending on the state you live in, this can be a far fetched question. In some states it's presumably as "simple" as getting a liquor license. In other states it requires millions of dollars and political connections. But unless you have experience as a farmer or have consistently produced quality Cannabis at scale, then wanting to open a dispensary is like opening a brewery just because you like beer. If you have experience or a competitive advantage and the team to implement and execute a system, then by all means go start a farm. Just remember that until banking regulations change you're going to have to run a business in cash and pay a ridiculous amount of taxes that you would not have to pay as a startup entrepreneur in any other legal industry.

By the way, remember the laws of supply and demand from chapter 1? They still apply. So as more Cannabis producers enter the industry, the supply of Cannabis increases and downward pressure is put on price. Data from legal markets indicates that the wholesale price of Cannabis has been decreasing over time.

> *"Find a niche and service it. Do what you do well in your corner of the sandbox. Expand out from there. You can't rule the whole box, it's too diverse. Look for ancillary opportunities and then expand."*
> **-Jerry Szycer**

Most of the people who benefited financially during the Gold Rush were selling picks and shovels. The total ancillary Cannabis market represents a bigger opportunity than producing and selling product. If you're a newcomer to this space, it is highly unlikely that you can earn success on the product side. There are farmers and extract artists who have *years of experience plus the relationships necessary to create the best product at scale.* Given the risk associated with businesses that "touch the plant" —reputation risk, lack of 280E exemptions, shortage of exit opportunities— it's likely that your best bet to add value and create a successful business is on the ancillary side of the industry.

Picks and shovels —or in this case, grow lights, legal services, nutrients, extraction machines, etc.— when all combined represent an opportunity that is larger than the opportunity in products. The Johnson & Johnson, Kraft, and Coca Cola of Cannabis product brands that emerge will all need grow lights, soil, testing services, packaging, etc. The ancillary market is open to proven business models and methods. With ancillary companies, you can access banking and all the tax breaks that businesses (and investors) enjoy! Although, please note that even ancillary businesses in Cannabis will face greater scrutiny when it comes to banking, compliance, and legal considerations than businesses in other industries --especially if you have Cannabis in your company's name.

Head over to www.Entrepreneur420.com/bonus to get a list of ancillary business success stories.

5.

Long Term Focus

"Have a real long view approach to it. There's not a lot of big players looking for acquisitions. Make sure you can last for the next 5 years. Don't give up. Things change rapidly. Hang in there."   **-Cy Scott**

Rome wasn't built in a day. Neither was the Internet. Legal Cannabis is no different. Many industry insiders agree that the end of Federal Cannabis Prohibition is at least 5 years away. It will take another 5 - 15 years for all the regulatory frameworks to be ironed out. If you're viewing Cannabis as a get rich quick opportunity, think again. The opportunities are immediate, but please don't enter this industry with a Gordon Gecko, *greed is good* approach. That's not what the Cannabis community is about. Frame your goals in terms of values.

What's your plan for growing your business? How will it adapt to changing industry dynamics? What is going to set it apart from your competitors? Clarity of purpose is important when you venture out on the entrepreneur's odyssey. There will be times of great stress, difficult decisions, and intense pressure. A compelling vision of what you want to contribute will help you push through those tough times. Why are you doing this? What's the true motivation? Start with why.

What's the exit strategy? Investors mostly care about one thing: getting a return on investment. Are you prepared to explain your long term plan?

Really define your goal. See it. Feel it. Champions visualize success. They prepare for it. They build towards it day by day, hour by hour.

Growing a business is tricky enough. Scaling a business in an industry that is simultaneously scaling is an even more dynamic exercise. What impact do you want to have? What is the long term relationship you want to create with your customers? How will that develop as the industry develops? What resources do you have at your disposal to make this happen? How do you want to contribute to the community? Make a list of your answers and keep it nearby so you can reference it in times of self doubt or uncertainty.

When the going gets tough what will keep you motivated? Studies of top performers show that they are motivated by a higher purpose or calling. They challenge themselves to serve a community, solve a problem, or change the status quo in a major way. What's driving you to take on the tremendous challenge that is Cannabis entrepreneurship?

6.
What's Your One Thing?

"What is your specialization going to be? What is that one thing you're going to do really well, better than anyone out there in this industry? Stick with it. It's very easy to get diluted and distracted, but focus. Stay focused. Perseverance is going to be the difference between the losers and the winners." **-Dr. Gerry Bedore**

"Find what your passion is in this space, and then stay in that. The Cannabis industry affects every part of the Gross Domestic Product. It's food, building, medicine and all the peripheral industries. It's so enormous. Find your passion and niche, surround yourself with other people who share that passion, and stick with it."
-Mara Gordon

One of the most common pieces of advice industry leaders gave was this: pick one thing and do it really well. Those are *literally* the Doctor's orders. Don't try to do everything. Cannabis is too big. There's too much ground to cover. In his book, *Zero to One*, Peter Thiel of Founder's Fund, co-founder of PayPal, early investor in Facebook, and now an investor in Privateer Holdings, makes the claim that the best companies are small monopolies. Build your small monopoly in some niche and defend it. Create something that will generate predictable revenue. To do so, you must be consistent in the product or service your business provides. You must have impeccable customer service and a commitment to excellence.

There is so much opportunity in Cannabis that eager entrepreneurs often claim (or make the excuse) that their greatest challenge is having too many opportunities to choose from. What you say "No" to is as important as what you say "Yes" to. Before making commitments or taking on new risks, think about your long term vision and whether or not the proposed actions bring you closer to or further from your end goal.

From a branding standpoint, it's a lot easier for your customers, fans, and partners to talk about you if they know you for one thing. For example, you hear the brand Raw and you think rolling papers. You hear the name Volcano and you're talking big bags filled with vaporized goodness. Make it easy for others to share your brand and your identity in the market places. How? By keeping it simple and doing one thing really well.

What impact are you going to have in the industry? What is your product or service good for? Simplicity scales. Can you answer the previous questions in one sentence? This is a revolutionary industry and the world is changing faster than ever before, what is your long term differentiator? How are you going to become irreplaceable in the Cannabis world?

7.
Expect Change

"Write your business plan in pencil, because when the laws change you better be ready to adapt and change with them." -**Greg Gamet**

Cannabis moves fast. Really really fast. Be prepared for change. Thrive in chaos. Rely on your values and build a network of compassionate, honest, growth-minded people.

8.
Embrace Failure

"I fail every single week in this industry. Every single day. Because there is no foundation for this marketplace. It's a matter of mitigating risk the best that you can. By having vision, what are you going to do, how are you going to do it, how will that affect the business?" -**Brandon Hamilton**

"Being really resilient is essential. There's a lot of opportunity for failure. You must dust yourself off and pick yourself up constantly." -**Christie Lundsford**

Persistence, grit, and determination are all muscles you will strengthen when exercising entrepreneurship. The only way to gain experience is by taking imperfect action and learning from the outcomes. There will be many times of uncertainty when, as the leader, you will have to make a tough decision. You have to accept upfront that you will get things wrong.

In coaching scores of entrepreneurs, I've noticed a dangerous pattern that beginner entrepreneurs often fall into. It looks like this:

1. Overanalyzing to try and find a perfect plan

2. An inability to execute quickly because of slowed momentum
3. Concern about the slowed momentum
4. Anxious second-guessing of the already overanalyzed plan
5. Deep frustration about the lack of positive results
6. Sadness, guilt, shame and loss of confidence

Having gone through that cycle more than a handful of times myself, I can tell you earnestly that it is not fun. No, in fact the best way to deal with that cycle is to avoid it altogether. Instead, give yourself permission to fail and be imperfect from the start. Thomas Edison famously joked "I have not failed. I've just found 10,000 ways that won't work." Ultimately he persevered, created the light bulb, and had tremendous impact on society with his innovation.

Success and growth occur outside the comfort zone

If you're not failing regularly, then chances are you're not taking enough big, bold actions. Make it a habit to regularly step beyond your comfort zone as an entrepreneur. Please note, I'm not saying to do anything crazy and then convince yourself it's for the sake of growth. Don't try to be a mule for a cartel because it's new and puts you outside your comfort zone. Don't compromise your values — that's the wrong kind of discomfort. But compromise on your insecurity, fear or inexperience. Write a press release even if you have never done it before. Produce a podcast even if you're not tech savvy. Attend a seminar on some segment of the industry you don't understand completely. Invest some money in your business or education. These types of visits outside the comfort zone will produce success even if it takes small failures forward to get there.

Nobody knows what's coming next in Cannabis, so don't get distracted by disagreement over where Cannabis is going. Everyone is entitled to their own opinions. But don't let someone else's skepticism or negativity influence your thinking. Allow yourself to experiment and test new ideas.

9.

There's Enough Green for Everyone

"There is $50 Billion dollars of Cannabis bought in the U.S. every year. Investors are coming into this space because you don't have to prove demand. You have to create regulations, best practices, and standards to serve the demand." **-Scott Greiper**

This opportunity is unprecedented. It's huge. Abundant. $50 Billion and growing. There's more than enough for you to make a very comfortable or even luxurious living. That's enough to create 50,000 millionaires in the next decade. Some of these new millionaires will become Cannabis venture capitalists and use their profits to fund the next generation of entrepreneurs and innovators. The point is don't be greedy. This community will not accept that.

So when you experience success and are in the position to lend someone else a helping hand or facilitate their success, please do it. Remember all the times someone —a mentor, a customer, a partner, etc.— went out of their way to help you. There's plenty to go around for everyone. Plus, you never know who someone will become in 5 years.

History has demonstrated that time and time again, Cannabis has been used as a political tool to push certain agendas. There is no doubt that even after Cannabis prohibition ends, there will be groups who fundamentally oppose this industry and culture. Thus, in the interest of protecting Cannabis values and culture, industry leaders must collaborate and support each other for the sake of the greater community.

Think again about what kind of Cannabis industry you want to co-create and participate in. What kind of world do you want to live in? What do you want the next generation to live like? Let that be your motivation. Act from a place of abundance, rather than from greed. Greed is the byproduct of fear.

Lastly, consider donating 10% of your profits to charitable causes and to activist organizations. Invest in the movement! This is especially important when you encounter success. You're not bound to your home state. There are several states that will be voting on Cannabis legalization in the next few years. Support the legalization efforts and the activists working hard to get the laws changed and allow the industry to grow.

Create an ethos of paying it forward and inspire

everyone you work with to practice the habit of charitable giving. When you're running a business, you're left with little time to lobby Congress, interact with politicians, and be an activist.

Fortunately, many talented, passionate people are working hard to make industry expansion possible by devoting themselves to activism. Honor their commitment by volunteering or donating to organizations, like the ones listed below, dedicated to ending Prohibition.

Drug Policy Alliance

National Cannabis Industry Association

Marijuana Policy Project

Students for Sensible Drug Policy

Patients Out of Time

Americans for Safe Access

Veterans for Medical Marijuana

Minority Cannabis Business Association

10.

Most Importantly: People & Results

"It's all about relationships in the Cannabis industry. You want to make sure you don't burn any bridges. Be reliable. Cultivate relationships. My first advice: be reliable and consistent. It's a small industry, everybody knows who follows through and who does not. This whole business was based on trust and referrals when it was underground. If you want to get into the inner circle, it's difficult--you have to build that rapport." **-Robert Calkin**

"The biggest thing I recommend is be genuine and meet people. Make connections and relationships. There are a lot of people who have been in this industry for a long time. It's your duty to honor them, respect them, and learn from them. There's so much history that happened to get us to where we are now." **-David Hua**

Cannabis is the original social network.

The plant has a unique ability to turn strangers into fast friends. It unites people. Do not underestimate this plant's ability to bring people together. Embrace and appreciate it if you want to succeed.

Entrepreneurship is a team sport. The quality of people you have relationships with and the quality of those relationships is going to be a significant — if not *the most significant*— determinant of your success. Given the vastness of Cannabis and the variety of the personalities and backgrounds it attracts, it's especially important to be critical of whom you do business with. Relationships are everything.

Business doesn't grow in isolation. Teamwork is absolutely necessary to execute anything effectively at scale. The best growers, processors, retailers, researchers, and investors don't do it alone. Cannabis is already incredibly diverse and complicated as an industry. Understand that both producers and consumers in this industry are used to being in the shadows. Trust is the ultimate currency.

Who's your connect?

It's all about who you know. Do you know the best growers? The researchers? The elected officials? The investors? Or, better yet, do they know you? How are you going to get their attention, trust and partnership?

Information Matters

There is still a great deal of information asymmetry in Cannabis. Until recently, this community and industry were designed to be out of sight and underground. Thus much of Cannabis wisdom is proprietary. Simultaneously, it's very difficult to verify information or personal backgrounds. Be extremely skeptical and always be thorough in conducting due diligence.

I've learned that the industry is not as large you might imagine. Those who have been around for a while know each other, or of each other, and they have an established way of doing things. Remember that in an unregulated black market, dishonesty or lack of integrity can get you killed. Discretion, respect, and loyalty are taken extremely seriously by the activists and operators who have fueled this industry's existence prior to this decade's wave of legalization.

Trust Issues

Due to the illicit history of this industry you're bound to run into some unsavory characters. Hustlers understand the opportunity in this booming marketplace. That's exactly why many dispensaries hire security teams of ex special forces for the transport of cash. There's no shortage of people who will try to take advantage of you. I believe the technical term is *shark*. Don't be a victim of someone else's half-baked idea or, even worse, successful con. In addition to the stigma, if you're in a business that "touches the plant," you're technically operating a federally illegal business. Be extra sure to work with people who understand the risks associated with that. Become a scrupulous judge of character or partner with someone who already is.

Friends and Family

Entrepreneurship is a demanding, stressful, and unpredictable as a lifestyle. Very few people will actually care about your stress and struggles. It is easy to become lost in the harshness of entrepreneurship. Through the many challenges, be sure to take note of the people around you who consistently offer support, help, and encouragement. Be sure to honor and thank them regularly. Include them in your celebrations and express your gratitude for their support. And for everyone else, the only thing they will care about is the bottom line.

Execute Excellently

That's how you create positive results, which is what people care about in business. While luck and timing are powerful variables, effort and attitude are within your control. Are you hitting your growth targets, revenues goals, and other KPIs? What value have you created? How do you measure results?

Peak performance is now well-researched and many resources are available to help maximize your productivity. When you develop a reputation for consistency, professionalism and high quality execution, business grows organically. Luck happens to you.

Creativity and ideas are great, but a track record of achievement is something investors can get behind. This is why it makes sense that many entrepreneurs I interviewed suggested focusing on one thing. If you're just focusing on one thing — and the many other things that go into running a business around one thing— you're more likely to reach a consistent level of excellent execution.

The Results That Matter Most

In no particular order:

1) What do the balance sheet and cash flow statements say about your business?
2) What are your customers saying about you?
3) How does the industry perceive you?
4) How do you feel?

In Cannabis business, memories are especially short. As innovation and competition accelerate, there is less attention being paid to what you've already accomplished. *What have you done for me lately?*

Teamwork Makes The Dream Work

The best laid plans don't mean anything without the team to execute them. I've already emphasized many times my belief that human capital, and therefore your network, is the most powerful and important asset to consider when building a Cannabis business. A team with diverse talents that is aligned around a mission can achieve incredible things. It's exciting and fulfilling to be a part of.

Evidence of Execution is Called Experience

If you are new, start with something. Create value. Solve a problem. Execute something and start creating a track record of success. Then, when you're looking for investment or talent or customers you can point to an ability to get things done.

Don't Mistake Being Busy for Being Productive

Just because you're working, doesn't mean you're coming closer to the desired results. Investors want to see it on paper. They want to see the spreadsheets, the models, and the plan before they even think about showing you the money. Having a plan is a key to remaining productive.

Leverage the 80/20 rule to keep your enterprise running lean and agile.

MENTORSHIP & COACHING

When you don't have a lot of experience executing the things you want to achieve, find others that do and leverage their wisdom.

This book is all about learning from the pros. When I entered Cannabis, I had no idea what I was doing. But I knew how to connect with people. So I interviewed the industry's top leaders across business, policy, medicine, activism, and more. This book is a culmination of that project and the desire to create a resource for Cannabis startups.

Mentors are Absolutely Critical

They will accelerate your learning curve, expand your network, and help you avoid blind spots. Plus in this industry, they might share with you the dankest buds you've ever tasted. Mentors should be people who you admire and want to be like. They are the people who are either living your dream life or who have already lived it. They are your models of success. If you don't have mentors, you should start by thinking about who you want to be mentored by.

Stand on the Shoulders of Giants

I've had the pleasure and honor of working with some incredible people to make this book happen. But beyond that, every professional achievement I've ever accomplished from J.P. Morgan, to Google to High NY, was influenced by powerful mentoring or coaching I received. Thank you to everyone who helped me grow along my journey.

Invest in Execution

Know when to bootstrap and go lean and know when to spend on professional help. Some details —legal, insurance, taxes— should be no brainers. Don't skimp on infrastructure if you plan on scaling your business. Many executives invest in and benefit from coaching. According to a study of senior executives at Fortune 1000 companies who received coaching, the average return was 5.7 times the investment. **Bill Gates, Eric Schmidt and many other prolific business leaders agree that "everyone can benefit from coaching."** Not only will you benefit from working with a coach, but you will also learn coaching skills which can be applied to develop and improve the performance of your teammates and employees.

In my coaching business, I work with entrepreneurs to create mindsets and habits of mastery. For more information on coaching, head over to www.Entrepreneur420.com/coaching.

There, you can book a time to speak with me 1-on-1 about your business.

The Future of the Cannabis Industry

High Ideas by Michael Zaytsev

There's a lot of transformation in store for Cannabis. Politics are still a huge part of the process. Sensible taxation and banking laws are still not in place as of this writing. Adequate medical research is still not being done in the U.S. The fight to re-legalize is far from over.

As someone who has studied Cannabis from the inside while learning from the top experts, here are some predictions of what will emerge in Cannabis in the next few years. Keep in mind, I don't have a crystal ball. I want to hear your thoughts on what the future of Cannabis looks like. Email me at Mike@Entrepreneur420.com

The Separation of Medical and Adult Use

The same way "Ancillary or Nah?" is a fundamental question today, "Medical or Nah?" will be the fundamental question of tomorrow. As more states come on board and Cannabis is rescheduled, or ideally descheduled, on the Federal level, Medical Cannabis will start to resemble other pharmaceutical products. Today we lack knowledge of proper dosage and how to apply Cannabis to address specific ailments. **Dosage control MUST become much more scientific and reliable.** This is incredibly important.

Right now, there is no agreement in the scientific or Cannabis community about what one dose of Cannabis is. How can we create a true medical product without research and a thorough understanding of dosage and effects? How can we educate medical professionals without having that information?

There is a small fraction of Cannabis users who are very seriously ill. They need highly concentrated doses administered in a way that accounts for their other medications and specific treatment plans. Children with epilepsy need to get consistent, clean, reliable Cannabis oil with predictable results. It is likely that the Food and Drug Administration will become the regulating body of Cannabis medicine. This is when you'll see Cannabis medicine available at your local pharmacy, in hospitals and in huge retailers like Walgreen's and CVS.

The adult use or "recreational" market (I prefer the term wellness market —in fact many activists frown upon the term recreational) will look much more like the alcohol industry. The wholesale price of flower will continue to decline. We'll have some highly corporate mega brands as well as craft-bud producers. You'll be able to buy prepackaged bud and infused products in dispensaries, grocery stores and at the farmer's market.

The Emergence of Big Brands

As the federal law changes, regional market leaders will be able to cross state lines and the best of the best will compete against each other on a larger, national playing field. Some companies — Marley Naturals, Leafs By Snoop, Willie's Reserve— are already trying to become the Coca Cola of bud. Eventually they will compete against big Canna —Philip Morris & Co won't be on the sidelines forever. However, cannabis consumers will preserve the tradition of counter-culture and will ultimately buy from whoever has the best products. Quality is king. The mom and pop, craft grower will never go out of style.

DIY Cannabis

Access to information and product will become easier and easier for consumers to access. Once consumers cross the education chasm and better understand the fundamentals of the endocannabinoid system and the versatility of the plant, a significant portion of the market will begin DIY experimenting. More and more people will begin cooking edibles at home, making their own tinctures and salves, and even begin growing their own plants. Other ingestion methods are going to become more common for the average daily consumer. People will become more precise and personalized in how they use Cannabis.

Most adult use markets have seen infused products (edibles) and concentrates take significant market share away from flower. The prevalence of smoking as an ingestion method will continue to decline; however, it will never go away. There will always be a cultural aspect that comes with rolling something, passing it around and putting it in the air. It is a sacred Cannabis ritual that will not go out of style. However, the convenience and discretion offered by vape pens and edibles will lead more consumers to turn away from combustion. After all, smoking does have adverse health effects.

More Corporate, More Professionals

As more states go legal and start making lots of money on Cannabis, more and more talented people will try their hand at Cannabis entrepreneurship. The level of competition is only going to get tougher. So if you're thinking about starting a business, now is the best time to do it! As more markets come online, there is less stigma and fear around being in this space. This will attract professionals from less controversial industries to get involved. Also, as more institutional investors and established corporations enter the industry, it will force other participants to raise their professional standards. Scott Greiper of Viridian often mentions that his biggest challenge as an investor is finding seasoned leaders who have experience running businesses at a high level rather than running businesses high.

High Tech

There will be some kind of technology innovation that will completely disrupt the Cannabis industry as we know it. Perhaps it will be some discovery about the human endocannabinoid system. Or some sort of exponential leap in the ability to customize and optimize the variety and user pairing. I believe there will be some previously unimagined seismic shift in the next few years that will transform the industry completely.

There is a group of researchers who are working on mapping out the Cannabis genome. The vast majority of consumers and most medical professionals still have no idea how the various cannabinoids interact with the endocannabinoid system.

Speaking of Tech, Hemp Will Save Our Planet

Hemp has over 20,000 documented uses. Henry Ford built a hemp car that ran on hemp fuel. Hemp is a super food and one of the best sources of plant based nutrition. It absorbs Carbon Dioxide from the atmosphere. It absorbs toxins from the soil. It can be used to build energy efficient houses, clothing, and much more. Currently, research is being done to create hemp super capacitors which can revolutionize anything that uses batteries. Hemp 3D printers will revolutionize manufacturing.

Humans Will Take Plants More Seriously

Once more of the benefits of the Cannabis plant are embraced and utilized, people will begin to explore other plants and their powers. Ultimately, Cannabis legalization will facilitate a renewed connection with and appreciation for nature.

The End of Prohibition

Cannabis legalization has passed the tipping point. As long as industry leaders and Cannabis consumers engage in the political process Federal Prohibition will end. This plant is the original social network and the business opportunity around it is the biggest thing for entrepreneur's since the birth of the Internet. Cannabis had been intertwined with human life for thousands of years. In the next decade, an additional 4 - 6 Billion people will get access to smartphones and an "always-connected" world. There will be Cannabis users in that group. How will legal Cannabis be advertised? Right now Google, Facebook, and other major marketing mainstays limit Cannabis content. This will change as the law changes. How long until we're watching Cannabis Super Bowl commercials?

Future Questions

What are we going to teach children about Cannabis? About pharmaceuticals? About healthy living? All of these issues are going to be deeply impacted by what happens with Cannabis. What happens to other controlled substances (specifically psychedelics) when Cannabis becomes legal? How will international trade disrupt the national Cannabis industry? How will drug cartels adjust to the legalization of Cannabis?

Cannabis isn't a gateway drug, but the Cannabis Revolution will be a gateway revolution.

It will impact medicine, agriculture, politics and more. This social movement is giving birth to a multibillion dollar industry. You're still early! But the clock is ticking. The industry is expanding everyday. Land is being grabbed, talent is being acquired, and money is looking for investment opportunity. The plant is growing, the business is booming. How do you want to grow with it? What are you waiting for?

Appendix:

Meet the Leaders

Alain Bankier is a founding partner in New York Angels, one of the longest running active angel groups in New York City. NY Angels has invested over $95 million in entrepreneurial ventures. The Former CEO of The Manischewitz Company, a leading international Kosher food brand, Alain is an early stage investor and entrepreneur and is a member of the ArcView Investor group

Ben Pollara, a founding partner of LSN Partners, provides strategic counsel to clients as they manage their relationships with local, state and federal elected officials. He also oversees LSN's grassroots and grasstops advocacy practice. Ben is a driving force behind the legalization effort in Florida.

Betty Aldworth is the Executive Director of Students for Sensible Drug Policy. In 2012, Betty was the spokesperson and advocacy director for Colorado's Campaign to Regulate Marijuana Like Alcohol, the first to make Cannabis legal for adult use. She served as deputy director of the National Cannabis Industry Association in 2013, where she was responsible for developing NCIA's then-nascent educational programming and framing the national conversation about the industry. Prior to her work in cannabis and drug policy, Betty spent a decade motivating and engaging volunteers as a non-profit leadership professional.

Brandon Hamilton is the CEO of WAM Oil, a Seattle-based innovative and savy concentrate producer specializing in all organic Co2 cannabis oil. WAM Oil was the first cannabis extraction company in Washington State to package, brand and market cannabis oil to patients. Brandon recognized the healing effects of cannabis oil when his partner was diagnosed with cancer.

Charlo Greene is a broadcast journalist and media expert turned activist and businesswoman who has emerged as a leading voice in the ongoing conversation about legalization, as well as diversity, in the cannabis community after garnering more than 100 million views online. Charlo became a recognized leader in cannabis activism in September 2014, when she punctuated her on-air report on the Alaska Cannabis Club with the bombshell that she was the club's founder and owner, proudly declared her activism and signed off for the last time with, "F*ck it, I quit..." Immediately following her exit, Charlo successfully led the charge in Alaska's 2014 effort to legalize recreational marijuana, securing Alaska's place as the third state in the nation (and first Republican-led state) to legalize usage for adults.

Christie Lunsford is founder of Endocannabinoidology, a consulting firm providing cannabis science, technology and education management assistance to businesses and individuals in the cannabis community. A cannabis industry veteran, Christie has served as a consultant during the licensing, development, and formulation phases of multiple Medical Cannabis Centers and Infused Product Manufacturers in Colorado, California, Illinois, Maryland and Washington State. Most recently, Christie helped a client navigate the complex regulatory process necessary to obtain one of the five medical cannabis business permits awarded in New York State.

Mrs. Lunsford is recognized as a founding member of National Cannabis Industry Association and Women Grow and was recently honored as 2015 Cannabis Woman of the Year at the 5th Annual Cannabis Business Awards.

Cy Scott Co-founder of Leafly and now CEO of Headset, a tech company that provides insight and education to the cannabis industry. Cy is a tech entrepreneur who went from a startup, to a national company, to a successful exit and new project. There are not too many people in the industry who have done that. Leafly is one of the most recognizable brands in Cannabis.

David Hua is an entrepreneur, marketer, problem solver, and catalyst. He is currently the CEO and co-founder of Meadow Care. Meadow's on-demand delivery service allows patients to shop online for medical Cannabis products and get access to quality medicine from the comfort of home.

Ethan Nadelmann was described by Rolling Stone as "the point man" for drug policy reform efforts and "the real drug czar." Ethan is widely regarded as the outstanding proponent of drug policy reform both in the United States and abroad. Ethan is the founder and executive director of the Drug Policy Alliance, the leading organization in the United States promoting alternatives to the war on drugs. He received his B.A., J.D., and Ph.D. from Harvard and taught at Princeton University for seven years. He has authored two books on the internationalization of criminal law enforcement and written extensively for academic, policy and media publications.

 **Evan Eneman**, along with Snoop Dogg and Ted Chung, is a founder and Managing Director of Casa Verde Capital. Casa Verde is a pioneering venture capital firm that makes seed and growth-stage investments in innovative, high-growth companies. Casa Verde has invested in cannabis media platform MerryJane, compliant packaging company FunkSac and delivery startup Eaze. Prior to Casa Verde, Evan spent 11 years with PricewaterhouseCoopers, advising Fortune 100 companies on enterprise IT, risk management, data security, privacy, regulatory compliance, and process improvement.

 **Greg Gamet** is the owner of the Denver Consulting Group. Greg has more than twenty years of business development, investor relations and cannabis regulatory experience. He is also co-owner of Kush Bottles Colorado, DANK, and Elm Properties.

Dr. Gerry Bedore is widely known as a thought leader in technology-enhanced learning models. He was a co-founder of Socrates Distance Learning Technology Group, and has published studies and books focused on online student success and completion rates. Gerry is recognized as having developed many of the most successful higher education online programs in the world. Gerry served in roles ranging from institutional president to assistant dean for doctoral programs. He is a member of the Cannabis Career Institute, is involved with cannabis agricultural development with Green Cures Inc., is serving in a leadership role for Cannabis State University, and is a U.S. disabled veteran.

Jack Cole knows about the "war on drugs" from several perspectives. He retired as a Detective Lieutenant after a 26-year career with the New Jersey State Police—fourteen in narcotics, mostly as an undercover officer. His investigations spanned cases from street drug users to international "billion-dollar" drug trafficking organizations. Jack is a founding member and for eight years was Executive Director of Law Enforcement Against Prohibition, an international organization representing cops, judges, prosecutors, prison wardens, and supporters from 86 countries, who know a system of legalized regulation of all drugs will remove the violence which is the result of drug prohibition. He currently serves on LEAP's Board of Directors, and is an international speaker.

Jazmin Hupp was named a "genius entrepreneur" by Fortune Magazine and a top businesswomen in the cannabis industry by Forbes. Jazmin i the Founder & CEO of Women Grow. Prior to entering the cannabis industry, Jazmin launched six companies in retail, eCommerce, business services, and media. Her core practice is customer experience design, which combines product design, branding, and business operations. Recently, she served as the Director of Digital Media for Women 2.0, which helps women start high-growth ventures. During her tenure, the brand expanded from the Bay Area to hold events across six countries for over 100,000 business women.

 **Jerry Szycer** Even before receiving his MBA from NYU's Stern School of management, Jerry created many successful companies -- everything from Kosher Sushi to home electronics. Jerry's latest endeavor, CouchLock Corporation, produces the first and best selling terpene infused drinks formulated to enhance the effects of cannabis. CouchLock has sold over 500,000 bottles since it's launch back in 2012. KannaBliss was written up in Ed Rosenthal's latest book, Beyond Buds. The company believes in giving back to the cannabis community and has sponsored many activists and educational events. Feel free to reach out anytime MFCEO@CouchLock.com He believes that we all rise by lifting others.

 **Larisa Bolivar**, Executive Director of the Cannabis Consumers Coalition, has over 14 years of experience as a trailblazer and pioneer in the cannabis movement. Her years of dedicated activism to cannabis policy reform and

fighting for the rights of patients and marginalized community members led to her creating the Cannabis Consumers Coalition. She works to bring attention to important cannabis consumer issues such as pesticides use and the involvement of big businesses, like Monsanto, and more.

Mara Gordon specializes in the development of cannabis extract treatment protocols for seriously ill patients in California. She is the co-founder of Aunt Zelda's and Zelda Therapeutics. Prior to that, Mara worked as a process engineer, helping Fortune 500 companies create intelligent software by utilizing the Rational Unified Process. Mara sits on the boards of Zelda Therapeutics, #illegallyhealed and New Frontier.

Rachelle Yeung co-hosts the podcast "This Week in Drugs." She began her drug policy reform work when she co-founded a chapter of SSDP at the University of Colorado Law School, and then worked closely with the historic campaign to legalize marijuana in Colorado. In

2013, Rachelle moved to Washington, D.C. to serve as a legislative analyst at the Marijuana Policy Project. Then she became the Government Affairs Manager for Vicente Sederberg, the nation's leading cannabis law firm.

Rhory Gould is CEO of the Arborside Health & Wellness in Ann Arbor, MI. A cannabis activist for 35 years and counting, he started what has become one of the top dispensaries in Michigan. He also was one of the first dispensary owners in the state to begin on-site testing of medical cannabis for potency. Rhory was recently honored by High Times as a recipient of the Trailblazer award for his dedication to activism.

Robert Calkin has more than 25 years of experience in the cannabis industry. Robert has helped create numerous businesses that are successful today. He is a delivery service expert and is sought after for training throughout the cannabis industry. He created Green Dot Delivery Service in Los Angeles in 1988, and that same year he was one of the original members of the

American Hemp Council with Chris Conrad and Jack Herer. Robert is the author of Starting Your Own Medical Marijuana Delivery Service: The Mobile Caregiver's Handbook, a bestseller in the cannabis industry. Robert is the founder and president of the Cannabis Career Institute, which opened in 2009, and Cannabis State University, established in 2010.

Robert Raich practices law in Oakland, California, where he specializes in medical cannabis law, business law, political law, and lobbying. A graduate of Harvard University and the University of Texas School of Law, he previously practiced law with Eber, Nakagawa & Kitajo in San Francisco and with the Federal Election Commission in Washington, D.C. He was the attorney in both of the U.S. Supreme Court cases ever to consider medical cannabis issues: United States v. Oakland Cannabis Buyers' Cooperative, 532 U.S. 483 (2001), and Gonzales v. Raich, 545 U.S. 1 (2005). Mr. Raich was a member of the California Attorney General's Medical Marijuana Task Force (Chairman, Caregiver Issues Subcommittee), and he has taught classes on medical cannabis to cadets at Police Department

Police Academies, as well as continuing education classes to other lawyers.

Scott Greiper is the President and Founder of Viridian Capital Advisors, a New York based financial and strategic advisory firm dedicated to backing and building market leaders in the emerging cannabis sector. Viridian provides capital raising and M&A advisory services to its clients, while its advisory practice provides board development, business development and strategic advisory services. Mr. Greiper is also President and Founding Partner of The Secure Strategy Group, a New York and Washington, D.C. based financing and strategic advisory firm dedicated to backing and building market leaders in the security, IT and communications technology sectors.

Scott Reach A stand out in the cannabis breeding community, Scott Reach is the mastermind and founder of Rare Dankness. As a Master Grower, award winning Breeder, and cancer

82

survivor, Scott's life work and love is deeply rooted in Cannabis and span more than 15 years. Rare Dankness has won over 50 awards globally for their genetics.

Steve DeAngelo is a cannabis leader who has inspired millions throughout his four decade career as a cannabis activist, advocate, entrepreneur and educator. Driven by his compassion for others, Steve has founded many successful socially responsible ventures including Harborside Health Center, the largest medical marijuana dispensary in the world. Steve is also Co-founder and President of the ArcView Group, a company formed to introduce investors to the cannabis community, and vice versa. To attract the best, brightest and most motivated entrepreneurs and investors for the next innovative American industry, Steve and his staff operate the ArcView Angel Investor Network. He is also the author of *The Cannabis Manifesto*.

ABOUT THE AUTHOR

 **Michael Zaytsev** is a Brooklyn based Leadership Coach and Entrepreneur. His family immigrated to America on 4/20/91. After graduating from Stuyvesant High School, where he first came into contact with Cannabis, Michael got a degree in Economics from Claremont McKenna College.

He went on to work as a financial analyst at J.P. Morgan and then moved to Silicon Valley to work in Brand Marketing and Software Sales at Google. After teaching a Leadership and Teamwork training class at Google, Michael became interested in coaching. After a few years in corporate America and after suffering from a traumatic freak accident, Michael decided to finally pursue his lifelong dream of Entrepreneurship. He moved back to New York City, earned his Professional and Master Coaching Certifications, and started a coaching business.

In addition to coaching entrepreneurs on sales and growth strategy, Michael began volunteering for High NY. Driven to contribute to the Cannabis movement, Michael used his skills and passion for leadership development to organize education and networking events. High NY has grown into one of the world's largest Cannabis Meetup groups. Recently, Michael had the pleasure of delivering a TEDx talk entitled "Thinking Differently About Cannabis."

When he's not coaching or serving the Cannabis community, Michael enjoys family time, fitness, good food, hip hop music and stand up comedy.

Connect with Michael on Twitter @HiMikeZ or on LinkedIn.

Email: Mike@Entrepreneur420.com

Thank You!

Made in the USA
Columbia, SC
25 July 2018